BUILDING
ON A
DREAM

THE
LEANING
TOWER
OF PISA

Nicole K. Orr

PURPLE TOAD
PUBLISHING

Printing   1   2   3   4   5   6   7   8   9

BUILDING ON A DREAM

Big Ben
The Burj Khalifa
The Eiffel Tower
The Empire State Building
The Golden Gate Bridge
The Great Wall of China

The Leaning Tower of Pisa
The Space Needle
The Statue of Liberty
The Sydney Opera House
The Taj Mahal
The White House

Publisher's Cataloging-in-Publication Data
Orr, Nicole K.
    Leaning tower of Pisa / written by Nicole K. Orr.
        p. cm.
Includes bibliographic references, glossary, and index.
ISBN 9781624693465
1. Leaning Tower (Pisa, Italy)—Juvenile literature. 2. Architecture—Vocational guidance--Juvenile literature. I. Series: Building on a Dream: Kids as Architects and Engineers.
  NA2555 2017
  720
                                        Library of Congress Control Number: 2017940579

eBook ISBN: 9781624693472

ABOUT THE AUTHOR: Nicole K. Orr has been writing for as long as she's known how to hold a pen. She is the author of several other titles by Purple Toad Publishing and has won National Novel Writing Month ten times. Orr lives in Portland, Oregon, and camps under the stars whenever she can. When she isn't writing, she's traveling the world or taking road trips. Orr has never been to the Leaning Tower of Pisa, but, like so many other places in the world, it's on her list.

CONTENTS

Chapter One
The Tower Experience 5

Chapter Two
The Mysterious Architect 9

Chapter Three
Location, Location, Location 13

Chapter Four
Early Ideas 17

Chapter Five
The Man Who Saved the Tower 21

Statistics 26

Chronology 27

Chapter Notes 28

Further Reading 29

Works Consulted 29

Books 30

On the Internet 30

Glossary 30

Index 32

One of the tower's most recent updates has been to polish the outside marble so that it glitters in the sun.

The Tower Experience

If you were a bird flying over the Square of Miracles in Pisa, Italy, do you know what you would see? Dozens of people would be doing a strange dance. Some would be bending over or jumping into the air. Others might have their hands over their heads, or even posing as if kissing an invisible partner. Who are all these people? They are tourists taking photos with the Leaning Tower of Pisa!

Over six million people visit the Leaning Tower of Pisa every year, yet more pictures are taken outside the building than inside.[1] Groups, couples, and individuals snap photos of themselves hugging, kissing, kicking, and even just holding up this tower. Their poses are often so entertaining, Pisans will sometimes take photos of the tourists taking photos! These funny pictures are then posted to social media sites. They show how these tourists spend their vacations—many without ever actually going into the tower itself!

Looking straight up, the top of the tower reaches 183 feet high. On the other side, it is 185 feet in the air. The tilt is harder to see up close, but from the inside, it is impossible to ignore.[2]

The Base of the Tower

Although most tourists do not venture into the tower, many do. Only 30 people can go in at a time, and even then, it's crowded. On the first floor is the Fish Room, named for the carving of a fish over the door. The Fish Room would feel small even without all those people, as it is only 24 feet wide.[3]

The stairs have been so worn down by feet, the stairs are no longer flat.

Climbing the Stairs

There are 297 steps from the Fish Room up to the belfry at the top. Visitors have 35 minutes to climb to the top of the bell tower and come back down again. This might sound easy, since the lean isn't very obvious at the bottom. As people climb, they pass windows that help light the way. Without these windows, it would be very dark.

One side of the steps is worn smooth by centuries of climbers. As visitors spiral higher, the lean gets worse. Gravity forces them closer and closer to the outer wall. By the time they reach the bell tower, their shoulder might be rubbing the wall's white marble.

The Bell Tower

The view of the city seen through any of the 16 arches at the top is amazing. The tilt is the worst here, at over 12 feet off center.[4] Many of the people might lean sideways or hold on to the arches for support. Most of them take photos with one of the seven bells. These bells are so large, a family of five could stand with their heads inside. This is

If the bells were all rung at the same time, the entire tower would vibrate.

NOT recommended, however. You don't even want to be standing next to these bells when they ring! If you were, you wouldn't be able to hear anything for awhile.

The Leaning Tower of Pisa has become one of the most recognized buildings in the world. Many people would be surprised to hear the tower's lean was an accident. Imagine visiting the Square of Miracles if the tower stood upright. Would people come to visit? Would they make funny poses with it? What would the shops sell? What would be on the postcards and key chains? The Tower of Pisa was not supposed to lean, but if it didn't, the city of Pisa would certainly miss it.

You might think the best way to fix the lean would have been to ask the original architect. What's the problem? No one knows who that was to do so.

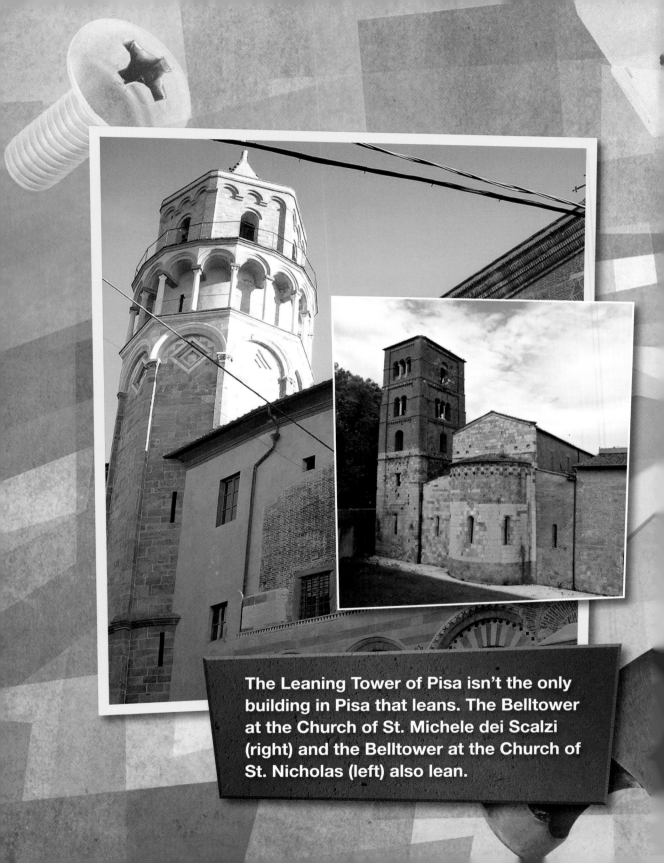

The Leaning Tower of Pisa isn't the only building in Pisa that leans. The Belltower at the Church of St. Michele dei Scalzi (right) and the Belltower at the Church of St. Nicholas (left) also lean.

The Mysterious Architect

When a little kid builds a spaceship out of Lego blocks, the first thing he or she wants to do is show someone what they did. The same applies to adults. When people build something important, they want to make sure that the whole world knows they did it. Architects love their work too, and they want people to know who built what. This is not the case with the architect of the Leaning Tower of Pisa.

Who Built the Building?

Bonanno Pisano was a talented Italian sculptor and artist in Pisa. He was well known for creating bronze doors for cathedrals. He was so famous for making these doors, he was brought in to make the doors on the new tower in Pisa. While he might not have been the mind behind the building, the tower must have been important to Pisano. When he died, he was buried at the foot of the very building he had been part of.[1]

Diotisalvi was another architect rumored to be behind the creation of the tower. There are similarities between the designs for the tower of Pisa and Diotisalvi's other projects. Two of those projects, the Church of Holy Sepulchre and the Belltower of St. Nicholas, also lean! There is, however, a catch. Diotisalvi always signed his work, and his name is nowhere to be found on the Leaning Tower of Pisa.[2]

While it took over 800 years for this structure to be officially finished, it is widely agreed that the basic construction was done in

In Medieval Times, nuns would cross the square on their way to their church. Around the time that construction on the tower began, people with aches and pains crossed the grass to visit the New Hospital of the Holy Spirit.

three stages over 200 years. The other 600 years were spent trying to correct the lean.

Many people were involved in building the structure. Some helped at the beginning. Some were involved in the end. Some were those who tried to fix the lean. Regardless of how many names have played a role in the Leaning Tower of Pisa, the identity of the original architect remains a mystery.

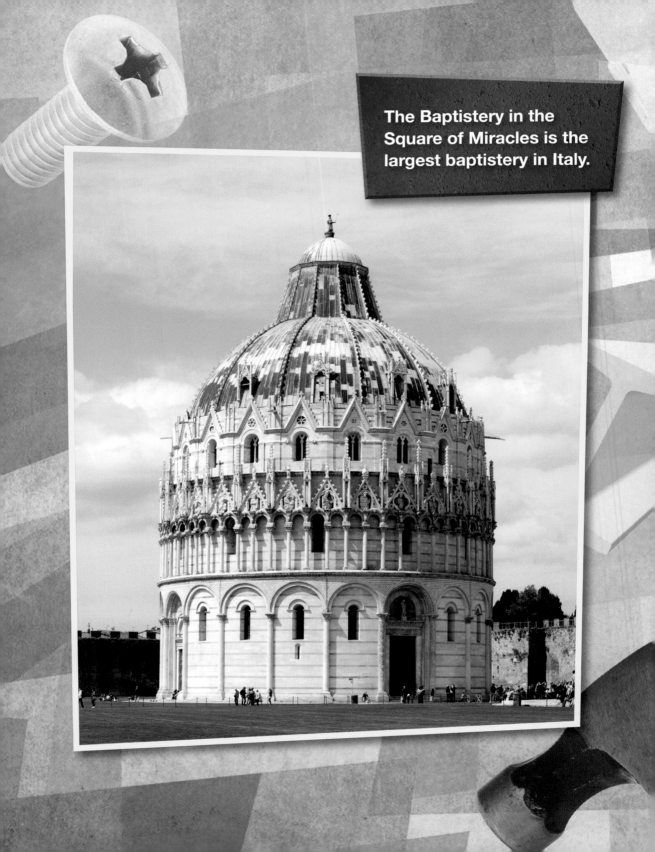

The Baptistery in the Square of Miracles is the largest baptistery in Italy.

Location, Location, Location

Construction of the Leaning Tower of Pisa began on August 9, 1173. It was to be a bell tower that would stand with three other buildings on a patch of grass called the Square of Miracles. The main building is a cathedral, with the tower alongside. There is also a baptistery and a cemetery. Together, they represent the cycle of birth, life, and death.

For the first five years of construction, the building was just called the Tower of Pisa. The lean didn't happen immediately. Some people wanted to blame the lean on the designs, but the problem was the location. The city of Pisa is located between two rivers—the Arno River and the Serchio River. Much of the ground, including where the tower would soon sit, was wet clay, sand, and shells. Getting this combination to support heavy buildings was a challenge.

Stage I (1173–1178)

The foundation for such a tall building should have been deep and sturdy. Modern engineers may have used pylons long enough to pass through the unstable topsoil and rest on solid rock. The tower builders did not do this. They dug down only about five feet, and they laid a solid foundation. That foundation was the foundation of their troubles.

On the first story, masons built the walls eight feet thick out of stone, lime, and mortar.[1] That level was built with no problems. It wasn't until the second story was finished that the tower began to lean. By the end of 1178, the third story was finished and the lean had worsened. Tests were done. The soupy ground could not support the

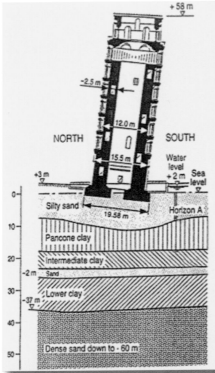

The soil under the tower caused the lean.

structure. Already, the subsoil was shifting—and the building was barely half finished! If the design plans were followed any further, the tower would topple. Because of the lean and the city's war with neighboring cities Genoa, Lucca, and Florence, architects and engineers agreed that construction of the tower must be postponed.

None of them realized that they would be postponing the project for almost 100 years.

Stage II (1272–1284)

The Tower of Pisa stood abandoned as the city suffered through war, harsh weather, and even earthquakes. All of this activity, while hard on the citizens of Pisa, was actually healthy for the building. The soil supporting the tower settled. This made the job of Italian architect Giovanni di Simone a little easier. He took one look at the project and knew what had to be done. When he added the final floors to the building, he'd make sure they were shorter on one side than the other. This way, everything would balance out.

Giovanni's plan did affect the lean, but not the way he had hoped. By the time he finished adding the final floors, it was obvious that the tower was leaning more than it had been before. Worse yet, it was now leaning in the other direction!

By 1284, the war with the neighbors had escalated again. With so much violence in the city, it wasn't safe for crews to continue construction. Workers went home. The tower was left alone again.

Stage III (1360–1655)

Tommaso di Andrea Pisano had the honor of putting a roof on the tower. He might not have been the one to design the original plans for the building, but he was the mind behind the belfry. Once the belfry was finished in 1372, the tower had a roof, and it was ready for its bells.

The bells are very large and very heavy. There are seven of them, one for each note of the musical major scale. The largest and heaviest, Assunta, weighs over three and a half tons. (It was not installed until 1655—nearly 300 years after the belfry was finished.)

Traditionally, some of the bells had a church-related purpose, too. Pasquareccia, as the oldest of the bells was called, was rung on Easter. The bell of San Ranieri, the Saint of Pisa, was rung whenever a traitor died.[2]

With the bells installed, the tower was finished. Approximately five hundred years had passed from when the foundation was laid to the installation of the final bell.

The full names of the seven bells are L'assunta, il Crocifisso, San Ranieri, La Terza, La Pasquereccia, il Vespruccio, and Del Pozzetto.

Because there is so little room inside the tower, the number of people allowed in at one time is strictly limited.

Early Ideas

From committees to teams to individuals, some of the world's smartest minds worked on the problem of the Leaning Tower. Some people questioned whether the lean should be fixed or only kept from worsening. There were talks of setting up nets and ditches in the ground below for when the tower eventually fell.

In 1838, Alessandro Della Gherardesca had an idea. He was digging a walkway around the base of the tower to uncover the parts that had sunk. He found that there was too much water underneath the tower. The ground was too wet to be supportive. Gherardesca used pumps to suck the water out of the soil. This caused a sudden shift in the earth, and the tower tilted more.[1]

In 1934, Italian dictator Benito Mussolini got involved. He thought having a leaning tower hurt Italy's reputation. He wanted the problem fixed, and suggested injecting cement into the base of the structure. The next year, engineer Giovanni Girometti put this plan into action. He drilled 391 holes and used pumps to inject the cement into them. Girometti also waterproofed the area surrounding the structure. He had sections of the floor removed and replaced with floor screed, which was another kind of cement. This was supposed to fuse the building to its base.

None of these changes made a difference in the tower's lean. The cement actually made the base heavier and made the tipping worse.[2]

Many other plans for fixing the tower were tried. Project Konoike was built on the idea of inserting chemicals into the earth in the hope

In 1964, cars could actually park in the shadow of the tower.

of stabilizing the soil. One of the craziest ideas was to take the tower apart and then put it back together in a better location.

In 1964, Italian Prime Minister Giulio Andreotti created the International Committee for the Safeguard of the Leaning Tower of Pisa. This committee of 14 included engineers, historians, and architects. One of these experts was John Burland. The only British man on the team, Burland was an expert on soil. He had helped save the Big Ben tower in London, England. That building had been on the verge of collapse also, but Burland had kept it standing. He hoped he could do the same for this tower.[3]

When the Prime Minister's committee took over, the lean was so bad, it was believed that even a violent storm could make the building fall. It wasn't safe to allow the public inside anymore. The Prime Minister decided to close the tower until a solution could be found.

In 1944, Leon Weckstein (left) was ordered to destroy the tower when it was occupied by German soldiers (above).

The possibility of collapse wasn't the only danger facing the tower. During World War II (1939–1945), a soldier named Leon Weckstein crept into the Square of Miracles. He was a twenty-three-year-old American soldier with orders to destroy the Leaning Tower of Pisa because German soldiers were inside. He tried to give the command to fire, but he was too taken by the tower's beauty to follow through with his mission.[4] Historians, tourists, and the many architects who followed have this soldier to thank that there's still a tower at all.

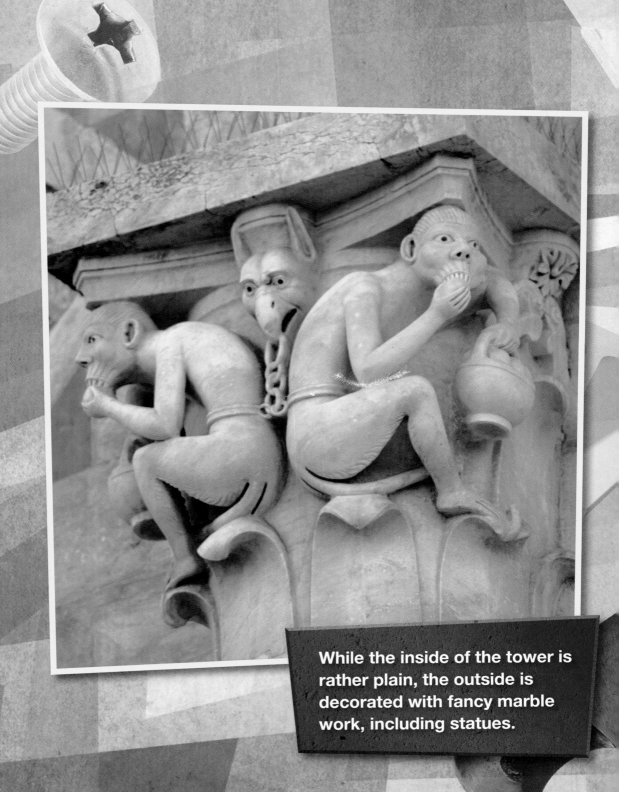

While the inside of the tower is rather plain, the outside is decorated with fancy marble work, including statues.

The Man Who Saved the Tower

During the closure—from 1990 to 2001—the Pisans grew very angry. Tourism to Pisa dropped severely. Shop owners, restaurant managers, and anyone else whose income depended on tower visitors were frustrated. They demanded that the tower be reopened, complaining that they were going to lose their businesses. The committee did not give in. The tower would endanger lives, not only of those who would climb it, but also of those on the ground below. Only one year before the closure, in 1989, another tower in Italy called the Civic Tower of Pavia had fallen. Four people were killed in that disaster.

Even with the tower closed, it was still a danger. Nearby areas were evacuated. Cables were attached to the third story of the tower and then to huge bolts driven deep into the ground. The bells had to be removed to lessen the overall weight of the building. These were temporary solutions. They would not save the tower or anyone near it if it fell.

In the ten years that they worked on the problem, the committee came up with a number of ideas. One suggestion was to attach big balloons to the top of the structure to hold it up. Another thought was to redesign the Square of Miracles so that the tower would look as if it were straight when it wasn't.

The members of the committee were constantly arguing. Some said the problem was in the soil. A few thought the building was to blame. Others said that they should not do anything to change the appearance of the tower or they'd be insulting its reputation.

While stacking lead onto the side of the tower didn't totally correct the lean, it did give crews more time to come up with something better.

The Prime Minister had forbidden the committee to tell anyone about their meetings, which happened only once every six weeks. To the citizens of Pisa, who were impatient to get their building back, it seemed that the committee was doing nothing at all.

In 1992, the committee took steel beams and used them to support the first story of the structure. It didn't work. In 1993, crews stacked lead on one side of the building as a counterweight. This didn't work either. Not only did these two efforts do little to affect the lean, but they also angered the citizens of Pisa. Pisans argued that everything the committee was doing was ruining what they loved about the tourist attraction in the first place.

The Black September

In 1995, the committee tried placing steel anchors into the bottom of the tower. To secure the anchors in the ground, they decided to freeze the soil using liquid nitrogen. Crews then drove the 10 steel anchors 131 feet into the ground.[1] The problem with this plan became apparent when the soil thawed. Gaps formed in the soil, and the tower sank down into those gaps.[2]

The committee called an emergency meeting in September of 1995. They were certain they were days away from losing the tower. Every time they created models based on the current state of the tower, the models fell over. There was absolutely no reason for it to still be standing. The committee was so sure of failure, this period was later called the Black September.

John Burland

The Solution

Finally John Burland had an idea that would save the tourist attraction. Even the citizens of Pisa couldn't argue with his plan.

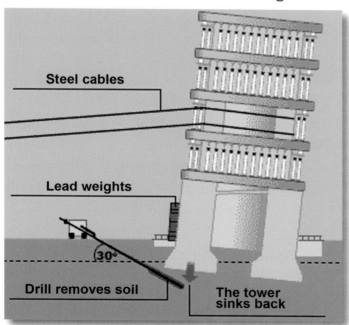

Steel cables

Lead weights

Drill removes soil

30°

The tower sinks back

In 1999, crews began a soil extraction operation. They used drills to make 41 holes and remove very tiny amounts of soil from beneath the tower on the side that wasn't leaning. Gravity did the rest of the work. With extra space on the side without the lean, the tower sank into the new space and straightened out.[3]

Burland said this about his solution: "The pressure was immense, a

When Burland first suggested soil extraction, crews worried that the tower was too unstable for such a risky idea.

modern wonder of the world was at stake—but I never doubted the logic of soil extraction."[4]

Burland's idea worked almost immediately. In the two years after crews began extracting soil, Burland had details of the tower and the earth below it faxed to him twice every single day. He would then send a fax back saying how much more drilling he thought was needed. At the end of two years, he had received 1,500 faxes, and 70 tons of soil had been extracted from the base of the tower. It was still the Leaning Tower of Pisa, but it was no longer in danger of being called the Collapsing Tower of Pisa. "We could have removed more," said Burland. "But our aim was to make the tower safe with as little intervention as possible."[5]

The building was reopened to the public on December 15, 2001, but Burland had a little more work to do. The first part was discovering the real reason the tower leaned. The answer was something Gherardesca had suspected back in 1838, but it was Burland who confirmed it. The amount of water under the tower was constantly changing. It pushed up higher on the tower's north side, forcing the tower to lean south. Burland had found the answer to the question that had stumped so many before him.

Now that he knew why it leaned, Burland knew what to do next. He installed a drainage system underneath the tower. This was to control the water in the soil, as well as how the tower shifts in that soil. Later tests would show that the tower did not move at all between 2003 and 2009. "It's stopped leaning completely . . . ," said Burland after his second success—and working on the tower for a grand total of 37 years. "The tower is safer than ever."[6]

Creating History

If you stood in the Square of Miracles today, you'd see quite a lot of people. There'd be tourists from all over the world, taking their funny

If you need ideas of how to pose with the tower that aren't holding it up, try pretending to give it a high five, a hug or even a karate kick!

photos with the tower. There would be students studying on the grass. Citizens of Pisa would be relaxing on the lawn as they enjoyed the scenery.

This site is getting more popular as time goes by. In 2017, a temporary Ferris wheel was to be added near the Square of Miracles. The city of Pisa hoped that tourists and locals alike would enjoy the attraction. If successful, the Ferris wheel would be made permanent.[7]

As you gaze at this magnificent structure, think about everything it took for this building to be standing here. Countless architects worked to create this tower, and at least as many worked to correct the lean. Every model, every computer simulation, every expert in the world would tell you that this building should not be standing here today, but it is. It has survived wars, weather, and bad ideas, all so that you could stand here and appreciate it.

Now go ahead and take a photo of yourself propping up the tower. You know you want to.

Height: 58.36 meters (191.5 feet)

External diameter: 15 meters (49 feet)

Weight: 14,453 tonnes (15,931 tons)

Greatest lean: about 5.5°

Post-2008 lean: about 4°, or 3.9 meters (12 feet) off center

Hewn stones: 29,424

Stone surface area: 7,735 square meters (83,260 square feet)

Capitals: 207

Staircase: 297 steps

Bells: 7

Stories: 8

Arches: Bottom story: 15. Each of the next six stories: 30. Top story (belfry): 16. **Total:** 211

1173   On August 9, crews begin construction of the Leaning Tower of Pisa.

1178   Architects realize for the first time that the tower is leaning.

1272   Giovanni Di Simone installs floors with one side lower than the other. He believes this will make the building curve until the top is level. Instead, it makes the tower lean the other way.

1372   Tommaso Di Andrea Pisano adds the belfry. When the bells are added, the tower is officially finished.

1838   Allesandro Della Gherardesca uses pumps to draw water out of the soil beneath the tower.

1935   Giovanni Girometti injects cement into the earth under the tower.

1964   Italian Prime Minister Giulio Andreotti creates the International Committee for the Safeguard of the Leaning Tower of Pisa.

1984   The Leaning Tower of Pisa becomes a World Heritage Site.

1989   The Civic Tower of Pavia collapses.

1990   Italian Prime Minister Giulio Andreotti closes the tower to the public.

1995   After many failed ideas, including using steel anchors, the committee loses hope. This is the time of the Black September.

1999   Soil extraction under the tower begins.

2001   On December 15, the tower is again open to the public. John Burland installs a drainage system beneath the tower to keep it from leaning again.

2008   Engineers declare for the first time in its history that the tower has stopped moving.

2017   Italian officials consider improving tourism to Pisa by installing a Ferris wheel as tall as the tower nearby.

Chapter 1

1. Ganga, Reena. "The Leaning Tower of Pisa Just Got a Little Bit Straighter." *Gadling*, October 31, 2013.
2. Mussio, Gina. "11 Things You Didn't Know About the Leaning Tower of Pisa." *Walks of Italy*. 2016.
3. "The Leaning Tower of Pisa." http://www.leaningtower-ofpisa.com/leaning-tower-of-pisa/
4. Arbeiter, Michael. "13 Straight Facts About the Leaning Tower of Pisa." *Mental Floss*, March 24, 2016.

Chapter 2

1. Leaning Tower of Pisa. http://www.leaningtower-ofpisa.com/leaning-tower-of-pisa/
2. Ibid.

Chapter 3

1. "Leaning Tower of Pisa." *Build Marvel*. January 2017.
2. Howlin, Julie. "Leaning Tower of Pisa." *Topical Tens*. July 2016.

Chapter 4

1. "Pisa Miracles' Square." *The Leaning Tower of Pisa*. http://www.leaningtower-ofpisa.com/pisa-miracles-square/
2. "Leaning Tower of Pisa." *The Leaning Tower of Pisa*. http://www.leaningtower-ofpisa.com/leaning-tower-of-pisa/
3. Smart, Alastair. "Solving the 800-Year Mystery of Pisa's Leaning Tower." *The Telegraph*. July 2010.
4. "Why I Spared the Leaning Tower of Pisa." *The Guardian*. January 2000.

Chapter 5

1. "Leaning Tower of Pisa: Brief Construction History." *Madrid Engineering Group*. http://madridengineering.com/case-study-the-leaning-tower-of-pisa/
2. Smart, Alastair. "Solving the 800-Year Mystery of Pisa's Leaning Tower." *The Telegraph*. July 2010.
3. Ibid.
4. Ibid.
5. Ibid.
6. Ibid.
7. Eustachewich, Lia. "Leaning Tower of Pisa Is Getting a Ferris Wheel." *New York Post*. March 10, 2017.

Works Consulted

Arbeiter, Michael. "13 Straight Facts About the Leaning Tower of Pisa." *Mental Floss*, March 24, 2016.

Carroll, Rory. "Why I Spared the Leaning Tower of Pisa." *The Guardian*, January 12, 2000. https://www.theguardian.com/theguardian/2000/jan/13/features11.g23

Eustachewich, Lia. "Leaning Tower of Pisa Is Getting a Ferris Wheel." *New York Post*. March 10, 2017.

Firusbakht, Leila. "Pisa and the Leaning Tower, at Sunset." *Tuscany Arts*, June 4, 2013.http://www.turismo.intoscana.it/allthingstuscany/tuscanyarts/pisa-leaning-tower-sunset/

Ganga, Reena. "The Leaning Tower of Pisa Just Got a Little Bit Straighter." *Gadling*, October 31, 2013. http://gadling.com/2013/10/31/leaning-tower-pisa-jstraighter/

Leaning Tower of Pisa. http://www.leaningtower-ofpisa.com/leaning-tower-of-pisa/

Leaning Tower of Pisa. http://www.towerofpisa.org

"Leaning Tower of Pisa: Brief Construction History." *Madrid Engineering Group*. http://madridengineering.com/case-study-the-leaning-tower-of-pisa/

McCafferty, Georgia. "Tilted Towers: The Secrets Beneath the World's Leaning Buildings." CNN.com, March 2, 2017. http://www.cnn.com/2017/03/01/architecture/leaning-towers-of-the-world/

Official Site: Piazza del Duomo in Pisa. http://www.opapisa.it/en/

Smart, Alastair. "Solving the 800-Year Mystery of Pisa's Leaning Tower." *Telegraph*, July 28, 2010. http://www.telegraph.co.uk/culture/art/architecture/7907298/Solving-the-800-year-mystery-of-Pisas-Leaning-Tower.html

Books

Armstrong, Simon. *Cool Architecture: Filled with Fantastic Facts for Kids of All Ages.* London, England: Pavilion Press, 2015.

Beck, Barbara. *The Future Architect's Handbook.* Atglen, Penn.: Schiffer Publishing, 2014.

Dillon, Patrick, and Stephen Biesty. *The Story of Buildings: From the Pyramids to the Sydney Opera House and Beyond.* Somerville, Mass.: Candlewick Press, 2014.

Kenison, Misti. *The Tiny Traveler: Italy: A Book of Numbers.* New York: Sky Pony Press, 2016.

Perkins, Chloe, and Tom Woolley. *Living In . . . Italy.* New York: Simon Spotligh, 2016.

Ritchie, Scot. *Look at That Building! A First Book of Structures.* Toronto, Ontario, Canada: Kids Can Press, 2011.

On the Internet

Cool Kid Facts—Italy
http://www.coolkidfacts.com/italy-facts-for-kids/

Facts for Kids—Leaning Tower of Pisa
http://factsforkids.net/leaning-tower-pisa-facts-kids/

National Geographic for Kids—Italy
http://kids.nationalgeographic.com/explore/countries/italy/#italy-coliseum.jpg

Time for Kids—Italy
http://www.timeforkids.com/destination/italy

PHOTO CREDITS: p. I—Jean-Paul Navarro; p. 4—Justin Ennis; p. 6—Jose and Roxanne; p. 8—Igorkon, Convolvolo; p. 16—Dave and Margie Hill; p. 20—Tammy Lo; p. 22—Rob Gerhardt; p. 25—Barney Moss. All other photos—Public Domain. Every measure has been taken to find all copyright holders of material used in this book. In the event any mistakes or omissions have happened within, attempts to correct them will be made in future editions of the book.

anchor (ANG-ker)—A heavy object used to hold another object in place.

architect (AR-kih-tekt)—The person who designs and draws plans for buildings.

baptistery (BAP-tih-stree)—A part of a church, or a separate building, in which people are accepted into the church community through a ritual involving water.

belfry (BEL-free)—The part of a building that holds the bells.

cable (KAY-bul)—A thick rope of wire.

casket (KAS-kit)—The fancy box or coffin in which a person is laid after passing away.

cemetery (SEH-meh-tayr-ee)—The land in which people who have died are buried.

computer simulation (kum-PYOO-ter sim-yoo-LAY-shun)—A model created and displayed on a computer.

counterweight (KOWN-ter-wayt)—A heavy load used to balance the weight of something else.

engineer (en-juh-NEER)—A person who designs and builds things, such as bridges, roads, machines, or buildings.

evacuate (ee-VAH-kyoo-ayt)—To quickly remove people from an area.

fax (FAKS)—A device used to send and receive documents over telephone lines; a document sent in the fashion; to send a document using this device.

intervention (in-ter-VEN-shun)—To come between in order to cause a change.

liquid nitrogen (LIH-kwid NY-troh-jen)—Nitrogen in its liquid form, which exists at extremely high pressure and low temperature. When the pressure is released, it turns into a gas that can freeze other objects instantly.

major scale (MAY-jer SKAYL)—The seven notes (A, B, C, D, E, F, G) upon which most music is based.

mortar (MOR-ter)—The binding material between bricks.

sculptor (SKULP-ter)—An artist who uses clay or other solids to create three-dimensional art.

soil extraction (SOYL ek-STRAK-shun)—Taking dirt away in a controlled manner.

reputation (rep-yoo-TAY-shun)—The general opinion people have of something.

traitor (TRAY-tor)—A person who suddenly turns against his or her country, friend, or cause.

translator (TRANS-lay-ter)—A person who takes spoken or written words and changes them into another language.

Alessandro Della Gherardesca 17, 23

Andreotti, Giulio 18, 22

Arno River 13

Baptistery 12

Bells 6–7, 15, 21,

Belltower of St. Nicholas 9

Big Ben 18

Black September 22, 23

Bonanno Pisano 9

Burland, John 18, 23–24

Church of Holy Sepulchre 9

Church of St. Michele dei Scalzi 8

Church of St. Nicholas 8, 9

Civic Tower of Pavia 21

Crocifisso 15

Del Pozzetto 15

Diotisalvi 9

Ferris wheel 25

Fish Room 5

Giovanni di Simone 14

Giovanni Girometti 17

International Committee for the Safeguard of the Leaning Tower of Pisa 18, 21, 22, 23

L'assunta 15

La Terza 15

Leaning Tower of Pisa
  arches 6
  belfry 6, 15
  bells 6–7, 15, 21
  foundation 13–14
  height 5
  sculptures 5, 20
  stairs 6
  tourists 5–6, 16, 21, 24

Mussolini, Benito 17

New Hospital of the Holy Spirit 11

Pasquareccia 15

Project Konoike 17

San Ranieri 15

Serchio River 13

Soil extraction 23–24

Square of Miracles 5, 7, 13, 19, 21, 24, 25

Tommaso di Andrea Pisano 15

Vespruccio 15

Weckstein, Leon 19

World War II 19